Contents

Christmas Where Santa Lives

Finland—the Arctic Circle land of ice and snow, northern lights, and reindeer. Home to a resilient people who delight in lighting the darkness of their long winter nights. Here, Christmas is a season of deeply spiritual—and highly spirited—celebration, plus plenty of fun in the snow. It's no wonder Santa makes Finland his home all year around!

From the glitter of their modern cities, to the glow of an Åland Islands cottage, to the welcoming fire in an isolated hut along a trail deep in the forest, to Santa's own snowy mountain home, the Finnish people welcome the world to share the warmth of their northern Christmas celebration.

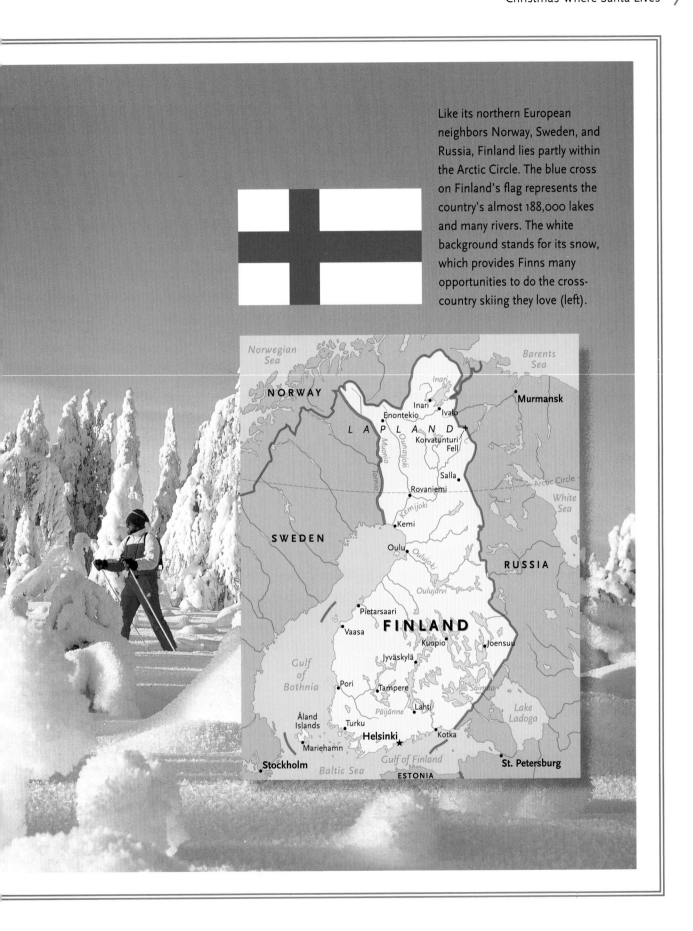

Like its northern European neighbors Norway, Sweden, and Russia, Finland lies partly within the Arctic Circle. The blue cross on Finland's flag represents the country's almost 188,000 lakes and many rivers. The white background stands for its snow, which provides Finns many opportunities to do the cross-country skiing they love (left).

Performing as dancing
Christmas gnomes,
children entertain a
crowd of Christmas
shoppers on "Christ-
mas Street" in the
center of Helsinki.

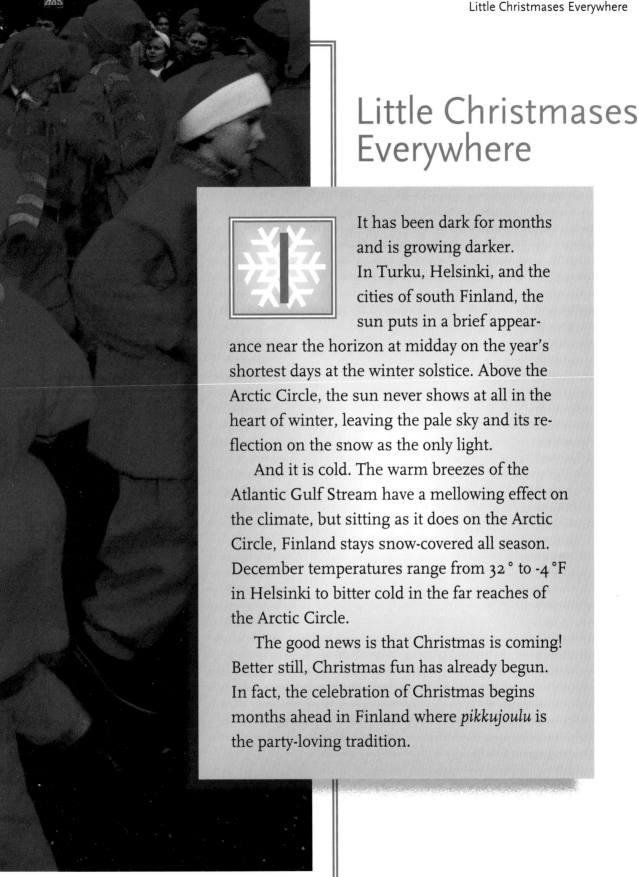

Little Christmases Everywhere

It has been dark for months and is growing darker. In Turku, Helsinki, and the cities of south Finland, the sun puts in a brief appearance near the horizon at midday on the year's shortest days at the winter solstice. Above the Arctic Circle, the sun never shows at all in the heart of winter, leaving the pale sky and its reflection on the snow as the only light.

And it is cold. The warm breezes of the Atlantic Gulf Stream have a mellowing effect on the climate, but sitting as it does on the Arctic Circle, Finland stays snow-covered all season. December temperatures range from 32 ° to -4 °F in Helsinki to bitter cold in the far reaches of the Arctic Circle.

The good news is that Christmas is coming! Better still, Christmas fun has already begun. In fact, the celebration of Christmas begins months ahead in Finland where *pikkujoulu* is the party-loving tradition.

Merry Little Christmases to All!

Lighting the darkness of December, Finns decorate their yards with candles protected by mounded snowballs (below). They also make ice lanterns to set out in the snow (below right).

Pikkujoulu means "Little Christmas," and it has meant Christmas fun and Christmas food ever since this Finnish holiday tradition began in the 1920's, when people began to have parties as they crafted things to sell at Christmas bazaars.

As early as October, the pikkujoulu parties begin. Women's organizations get together to make Christmas decorations, plan their upcoming Christmas bazaars, and have fun. Then everyone else follows suit. Churches, businesses, clubs, schools, towns, neighborhoods, teams. Every group joins in.

Traditionally, pikkujoulu parties center around a Christmas program, talk, play, games, or music. Always, they feature plenty of delicious Christmas food and drink, turning a long, dark period into a happy holiday season.

Counting the Days

Though the holiday celebration already has arrived by Little Christmas, the official opening of the Christmas season comes on the first Sunday in Advent, four weeks before Christmas. Everywhere churches

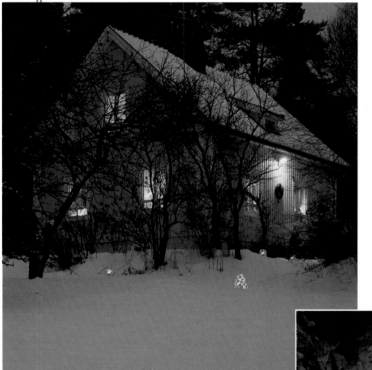

are crowded as people come to hear the traditional strains of Christmas hymns and to see the first Advent candle lighted in the church.

The Finns like to light their dark winter world with candles. Candles are a focus of holiday decorations in their homes. Out in the yard, candles are tucked inside mounds of protective snowballs or lanterns made of ice to light the night.

It is only natural that Advent candles are one of the most heartfelt symbols of Christmas here. The four Advent candles stand together along the circle of a wreath or in a line. The first candle is lighted on the first Sunday of Advent and symbolizes the

This Finnish boy enjoys his special Advent calendar with a trinket for each day of the season.

anticipation of Christmas. An additional candle is lighted on each Sunday leading up to Christmas, representing in turn Christmas joy, peace, and love. In Finland, Advent candles are in every church and nearly every home.

Advent calendars are a popular way to count the days until Christmas. They are sold everywhere in Finland, and they come in all sorts of clever variations. There are simple illustrated calendars with small pictures or Bible verses behind each flap that opens, elaborate wooden calendars that hide an ornament or chocolate treat in each compartment, numbered boxes filled with surprises hanging on the branches of a little Christmas tree, and all kinds of imaginative homemade variations. Finnish parents take great delight in providing this bit of Christmas fun for their children.

A season of Christmas concerts begins now, too. Churches large and small hold concerts and evening songfests during Advent to raise money for charities. They open their doors and welcome everyone to come join in singing carols such as *Enkeli taivaan* (Heavenly Angel), which has been a standard of the season since the 1600s.

Other Christmas favorites include carols written by Finland's own Jean Sibelius, such as *En etsi valtaa loistoa* (Christmas Prayer), which sets to music a holiday poem written in 1887 by Sakari Topelius.

St. Ann's Day

> The most important job of the day was baking the Christmas loaf.

Ann, the mother of Mary and grandmother of Jesus, became a Catholic saint who touched the heart of Finland. Often depicted wearing a green cloak and holding both Mary and Jesus on her lap, this motherly figure seemed familiar to the forest-dwelling Finns. Ann, for them, became also Anni or Annikki, the green-garbed, much-loved spirit of the forest who was said to protect wild animals and livestock.

In Finland, St. Ann's feast day on December 9 was traditionally the day women began their Christmas baking, cleaning, and brewing in earnest. Women rose early to bake and bake, making bread for their own families and for the poor.

The most important job of the day was baking the Christmas loaf. Limited only by the size of the oven, this huge round and flat loaf would serve as the base of the table's centerpiece throughout the holiday season. The bread would be stamped with the shape of a cross on top. Other smaller loaves would be stacked on this loaf, and a small round of cheese holding a candle placed on top. Sometimes, little rolls were fashioned as "feet" for the Christmas loaf so that crumbs could be dusted away during its long sojourn as a centerpiece.

During the holidays, the top loaf might be eaten and replaced, but the rest of the tower remained. When the holiday season ended, the Christmas loaf was saved to be eaten on the first day of planting and fed to the cattle as they were led out to pasture.

A tradition rooted in pre-Christian custom, the Christmas loaf was invested with the power to bring a good harvest and to protect a farm's livestock in the year to come. Some people were careful to

Baking is a large part of every Finnish Christmas. Here a grandmother and granddaughter shape loaves before baking.

reserve the first grain harvested to make the Christmas loaf each year. By eating the bread during the next crop's planting season, they symbolically carried a good harvest from one year to the next.

Although many families still make the Christmas loaf centerpiece, the present-day Finnish Christmas loaf is *limppu*. Playfully decorated with stars and holiday shapes cut from gingerbread dough, this sweet treat warms the Christmas kitchen air with a delightful mixing of orange, fennel, and cumin flavorings.

The Festival of Lucia

The history of Finland is intertwined with that of Sweden. Today, a solid 6.5 percent of the population of Finland, mostly living in the Åland Islands and the southeast portion of Finland, speak Swedish as their first language. Many more take pride in their Swedish heritage and customs. Some cities, such as Turku—called Åbo in Swedish—are identified by both Finnish and Swedish names. Other places, like Åland (Ahvenanmaa in Finnish) are known primarily by their Swedish names.

It comes as no surprise that Sweden's standout Christmas tradition, the festival of Lucia, has become a highlight of the holidays in Finland as well.

Celebrating the traditional Lucia Day, Lucia and her court are presented to the public with flowers and many lighted candles.

The festival honors a young Sicilian girl, Lucia, who suffered a martyr's death in 304 A.D. for converting to Christianity against her family's wishes. According to custom, a teen-age girl serves as the Lucia for her family. Crowned with a wreath bearing lighted candles and wearing a pure white dress with a red sash, she brings coffee and rolls to her family and presides over the breakfast eaten in her honor.

Lucia Day is celebrated on December 13, when the dark of night seems to have overtaken day in this northern land. The very first Lucia maidens wore wings as part of their costume. These were quickly replaced by the crown of candles, but Lucia retained her image as an angelic being who brings hope, charity, and light to brighten the darkest days of winter.

In Finland, some Swedish families began celebrating Lucia Day in the early days of the 1900's. In 1927, Sweden held its first Lucia competition, which is similar to a beauty pageant. In 1930, Finland selected its own national Lucia and celebrated with a parade in Helsinki.

Still, it wasn't until 1950 that Lucia Day became a real part of the Christmas season celebration in Finland. That year, Finland's principal Swedish-language newspaper, *Hufvudstadsbladet*, promoted the competition in conjunction with the health organization Folkhälsan as a charitable event.

Now a teen-age girl is selected each year by popular vote to be Finland's Lucia. Money raised is used to support health care programs. During her "reign," Lucia makes appearances at public events and visits schools and hospitals, bringing her message of light and charity.

Lucia's good works, along with her charm and beauty, have earned her a place in hearts all across Finland. Even Finnish-speaking families now often celebrate December 13 with a Lucia breakfast of coffee and saffron rolls served by a lovely daughter.

Clean and Ready

In Finland, the period of Christmas peace original-ly began on St. Thomas's Day, December 21. By this day, all the baking and brewing was finished. Houses and barns had been cleaned and swept from top to bot-tom, and Christmas candles for home and church were made. Now it was time to stop work, stop fighting, stop all nonsense, and turn attention to Christmas.

> The more it snows before St. Thomas's Day, the better the crops in the year to come.

St. Thomas's Day provided another opportunity to cast ahead and scout conditions for the coming year. According to Finnish folklore, "The deeper it piles up before Thomas's Day, the deeper it piles up in the bin," meaning the more it snows before St. Thomas's Day, the better the crops in the year to come.

Star Boys Light the Night

In some parts of Finland, particularly around Oulu and in southwest Finland where they are called "star boys," small groups of boys once roamed the city and countryside during the weeks surrounding Christmas, singing carols or acting out skits.

Today, boys and girls carry on the tradition in a limited way, appearing only at special events during the holidays. The children may be costumed as wise men or angels, and they carry a large candle-lit paper Star of Bethlehem. These young performers brighten the season in schools, hospitals, and other Christmas functions with their traditional Christmas greeting:

"A good evening, a good evening to all of every degree, and to our host and hostess, and we wish you, and we wish you a merry and fair Christmas."

A Finnish family makes traditional Christmas ornaments of straw. Hanging in the window is a himmeli.

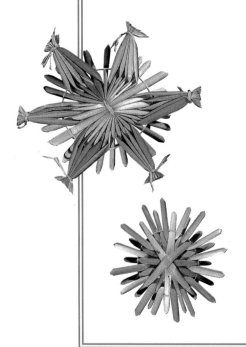

Natural Beauty at Christmas

Natural materials, often combined with a red ribbon or bow, figure prominently in Finnish Christmas decorations. Straw especially became associated with Christmas because in ancient times straw was often used in rituals that helped predict or ensure fortune in the next year's harvest.

The most cherished Christmas decoration in a Finnish home is the *himmeli*, an intricate geometric mobile crafted by hand from twisted straw pieces. The name himmeli is from the Swedish word for heaven. Another Finnish name for the himmeli was *olkikruunu*, or "straw crown."

To make a himmeli, first the finest quality of very straight rye straw is selected. The straw is then softened in the warm, moist air of the sauna and cut into sections. Women experienced in this complicated craft bend and twist the straw into triangles, squares, and eight-sided figures, combining many pieces into a fantastic design.

In the past, himmeli-making bees were an Advent tradition. Skilled young women would sit in the changing room of a sauna, making the lovely decorations in the moist air. Young men came to watch, and the himmeli bees quickly turned into parties. By tradition, the himmeli was made at Christmas and remained hanging in the home's main room throughout the following year. Now, himmelis hold the place of honor in Finnish homes during the holiday season.

The Finns also use straw to make other ornaments and standing figures of stars, reindeer, elves, and other Christmas characters. They fashion wreaths of straw and grain for the door. Wood shavings, too, are formed and molded into stars and other imaginative shapes.

In many homes, a lovely Christmas bird hangs above the dinner table. Once rare, this increasingly popular Christmas decoration symbolizes the Holy Ghost. The Christmas creche, popular around the world, also has become an element of Christmas in some Finnish homes and a part of public holiday decorations.

In pagan times, the season now associated with Christmas was a time when evil spirits were said to roam the countryside, menacing people and animals. Some present-day Finnish Christmas decorations originated then as protective signs to ward off trouble. And later some Christian decorations, such as the Cross of (St.) Thomas, or Korppoo Cross, were enlisted as good protection from evil. Some people hung the cross in a window; others used tar to paint protective crosses above their doors.

Straw and wooden ornaments are often made in the shape of stars, crosses, and reindeer.

In this historic photograph, a Finnish girl enjoys her Christmas tree decorated with paper ornaments (below). A triumphant father and son head home with the Christmas tree they have cut down in the forest (below right).

The Finnish Tree

Most sources agree that the Christmas tree arrived in Finland in the 1830's in the Helsinki home of Professor Alexander Blomqvist, whose German wife brought the custom from her homeland. By other accounts, the Finnish tree arrived earlier and came in a crowd. For Christmas 1829, Helsinki nobleman Baron Klinckowstrom is said to have had eight lighted trees in his home.

Whatever the year and no matter how many, the Christmas tree had come to stay. Other well-to-do families quickly added trees to their Christmas decor. Next, school and social organizations had Christmas trees. By the turn of the century, Christmas trees were standing proudly in the homes of the rich and poor, in the cities and the countryside all over Finland.

Finnish Christmas trees have always been decorated with candles, although now wax candles are generally replaced by safer electric ones. Early Finnish trees were decorated with gingerbread cookies, paper roses, nuts, candies,

and apples. Over time, homemade decorations gave way to glass beads, glass bells, and birds. Often, a ribbon reading "Glory to God in the highest, and on Earth peace, good will toward men" was wrapped around the tree as well. There was always a star on top.

Today there are lovely handmade Finnish straw decorations of snowflakes, reindeer, stars, and other Christmas shapes glowing in the light of tiny candles. Angels, bells, and glass ornaments are found on many Finnish trees. In addition, it is customary to dress the tree in a garland of little flags from Finland and other countries all over the world. The garland symbolizes both Finnish pride and a wish for brotherhood among countries.

When the Finns took in the Christmas tree, they took celebration trees to heart. In southwestern Finland, decorated trees began to show up all year around. In Finland, it is customary to celebrate each new year of a person's life not on their birthday, but on their name day—originally a saint's day, but now simply the day assigned to all people with a certain name. On your name day, you are likely to wake up to find a small spruce tree with presents for you hanging on it.

> **By the turn of the century, Christmas trees were standing proudly in the homes of the rich and poor, in the cities and the countryside all over Finland.**

City Lights Shining Bright

Christmas arrives with a blaze of holiday lights just before Advent in cities big and small across Finland. Often an Advent parade and street lighting ceremony open a city's festive holiday season.

In Helsinki, Santa Claus and Mrs. Claus arrive by steam locomotive to start the holiday parade to the square where the city's mayor will declare the official Christmas street open.

Aleksanterinkatu has been Helsinki's Christmas street since 1947. It is here that lights are strung in profusion. And here shoppers come to enjoy some of the city's many wonderful open-air Christmas bazaars, for all those pikkujoulu decorations and tasty treats are now for sale.

One of the best is the popular *Tuomaan markkinat* (Thomas's Market) in Helsinki's Esplanade Park. Here, nearly 100 stalls offer Christmas handicrafts, confections, and delicacies. There is plenty of warm, spiced wine and delicious sausages to try. Santa himself can't resist showing up for a taste or two. This major bazaar is only one of several held every Christmas in Helsinki alone.

Downtown Helsinki is brightly decorated with traditional Christmas lights. Short December days make the lights even more welcome.

Christmas bazaars spring up in the center of nearly every Finnish town. The sale of crafts and foods often benefits worthy charities. The treats brighten homes everywhere as the holiday season begins.

In addition to its Santa Claus and Lucia Day parades, plus a very full schedule of holiday music concerts at all the city's major churches, Helsinki decorates historic homes in the traditions of Christmases past and hosts family-centered holiday events at its zoo and museums.

Turku calls itself Finland's Christmas City—a name it earns every year. Turku is the city where the Proclamation of Christmas Peace is read, a city where Christmas traditions are held dear.

Like Helsinki, Turku starts the holiday season with a grand lighting ceremony and the opening of its traditional Christmas Market. In Old Market Square, vendors dressed in period clothing sell mulled wine, coffee, and traditional Christmas rice porridge with raisin soup to warm shoppers strolling amid numerous evergreen-trimmed stalls. Turku residents and visitors from around the world look forward to this fair each year and the chance to sample Christmas favorites such as gingerbread cookies and rutabaga casserole, buy Christmas decorations or clothing, check out the fishermen's stall, visit with Santa himself, and enjoy a circle dance around the city Christmas tree.

At Turku Castle and several of the city's historical museums, period Christmas dinners are held with menus and decorations that take the celebrants to Christmases past. At Qwensel House, built at the beginning of the 1700's, a decorated carriage shed is the site for a Lucia Day reception with mulled wine from a secret household recipe.

There are also numerous Christmas concerts by the Turku City Orchestra and at various churches, and Christmas craft workshops of all kinds for children.

On Finland's west coast, the town of Pietarsaari first lit the night with Christmas decorations in the 1840's. The town's cherished decorations—a giant cross symbolizing faith, an anchor for hope, and a heart representing love—hang suspended over the main street, lit earlier by traditional candles and now by electric ones. The beautiful, simple symbols have been shining brightly every Christmas since, interrupted only briefly by wars and saving energy during the oil crisis of the 1970's. Pietarsaari is also credited as the first city in Finland to stand a Christmas tree decorated with electric lights in its town square.

In the Åland main city of Mariehamn, the Finnish traditions are played out with island charm. Merchants on the "Christmas Street" here offer handicrafts as well as Åland dark bread and local Christmas foods. Lucia Day is extra special here, celebrated with a big torchlight parade marched in by children. And there are, of course, many Christmas concerts offered by local churches.

In Rovaniemi, the Lucia Day parade sometimes winds its way through town to end at a special reception in Santa's Workshop. Children visiting this Christmasy world from other countries are welcomed to join in the parade and the fun.

In the city of Turku, the traditional Christmas Market takes place every year. Vendors decorate their stalls and string bright lights between them.

The Peace of Christmas

People gather to listen to the annual Proclamation of Christmas Peace in Turku (right). On the balcony of Brinkkala House, the town clerk reads the Proclamation to the assembled crowd (below).

decked in glowing holiday candles, he holds in his hands an unrolled parchment scroll bearing the proclamation and the seal of the city.

As the bells of Turku's nearby 700-year-old cathedral strike 12, the town clerk reads:

"Tomorrow, God willing, is the graceful celebration of the birth of our Lord and Savior; and thus is declared a peaceful Christmas time to all, by advising devotion and to behave otherwise quietly and peacefully, because he who breaks this peace and violates the peace of Christmas by any illegal or improper behavior shall under aggravating circumstances be guilty and punished according to what the law and statutes prescribe for each and every offense separately. Finally, a joyous Christmas feast is wished to all inhabitants of the city."

The Proclamation of Christmas Peace was first read sometime in the early Middle Ages.

At exactly noon on Christmas Eve, all of Finland stands still, listening. In Turku, a crowd gathers in front of Brinkkala House. Elsewhere, families turn on the radio or gather in front of the television set. Now, with the Proclamation of Christmas Peace, the holiday truly will begin.

The town clerk of Turku stands on the balcony of Brinkkala House, an elegant old stone house. Flanked by two impressive fir trees

Before long, it became a holiday tradition throughout the Scandinavian world. By the 1200's, the Proclamation was being read each year in every town under Swedish rule, including much of Finland. Today, only Finland continues the tradition.

The proclamation originally was intended to squelch rowdy behavior and serious mischief-making during what could often become a wild and raucous season of celebration. The occasion of proclamation also was used to announce certain rules or restrictions that would be enforced. For many years, merchants officially were instructed to suspend all commerce from that moment for the celebration of Christmas. Later, in reaction to holiday fire tragedies, citizens were forbidden to spread straw on their floors as part of their holiday decoration.

In ancient times, as many as 27 different periods of peace might be called in a year. Along with the Peace of Christmas, there were times of peace proclaimed in relation to the harvest, court sessions, or other events of community life.

The modern reading of the Christmas proclamation has been enacted in Turku each Christmas since 1935. The proclamation read there today is based on an edict issued by Queen Christine sometime in the 1640's.

Turku is also called Åbo, the name given to the city by the Swedish who dominated this part of Finland for centuries. Until 1812 it was the capital of Finland. It remains one of the country's most historic and beautiful cities and the perfect setting for the reading of the proclamation.

Brinkkala House itself is an impressive stone building that over the centuries has served as the home of several families, as the city's Court of Appeals, as the Finnish president's residence, and as the Town Hall. Today it is Turku's Cultural Center.

The traditional blessing of Christmas peace extends even to animals. According to tradition, hunters this day must put down their weapons and let the wild moose, elk, lynx, and bear roam safe under the protection of the Christmas peace.

Also on this day, the secular Proclamation of Christmas Peace is joined by a separate but related religious call for peace coming from the leaders of Finland's major religions. Standing together in Turku Cathedral, the archbishops of the Evangelical Lutheran and Orthodox Churches and the bishops of the Roman Catholic and Methodist Churches raise their voices to issue an ecumenical appeal for peace. Through this annual joint statement, the Finnish religious leaders call on all people to remember the Christmas message of hope and peace for the world.

The proclamation of Christmas Peace is written on a parchment scroll.

A Family gathers in their brightly decorated home for Christmas Eve dinner. The baby is dressed as a Christmas gnome in a traditional red costume.

Christmas at Last!

With the Proclamation of Christmas Peace on Christmas Eve day, the Christmas holiday officially begins throughout Finland. Shops are closed. No last minute shoppers here! Families who have gathered to listen to the proclamation together now turn to their own celebrations.

In Finnish homes everywhere, final preparation is made for the holiday celebration. The himmeli is hung in a prominent place; there may be straw stars in the windows. Little straw figures of reindeer, goats, or elves are arranged in a playful scene on a table.

In the past, loose straw would now be strewn about on the floor. In Christmas tradition, the straw is a reminder of the stable and manger where Jesus was born. Before that, the custom dates back to pagan times when straw spread on the floor was intended to help assure a good crop in the year ahead. Because of the danger of fire, this is no longer done.

Candles, both inside and in front of the house, shine like glowing ice. Presents, other than those *Joulupukki*—Finnish for Santa—will bring, are arranged under the Christmas tree.

Flowers are arranged on the table. There may be snow outside and frigid temperatures, but there are always fresh flowers in the house at Christmas, and flowers are a gift for any hostess. Living in their land of abundant lakes and forests, the Finns treasure the beauty of nature. It would be unthinkable to celebrate without fresh flowers. Red tulips or hyacinths are popular choices. There are pots and baskets bearing all kinds of blooms.

Everything is ready. Now families can sit down to enjoy the first of two Christmas Eve feasts, a sampling of good things to come. Some families eat their main meal right after the proclamation is read, but most reserve it until late afternoon or evening.

The afternoon and early evening are the time for a Christmas Eve sauna and a special visit to the cemetery, the two most treasured of all Finnish Christmas traditions. The focus for all the meaningful events this day is family. Christmas Eve in Finland is a time to be in your own home, surrounded by your loved ones.

The two real obligations of Christmas Eve lie just ahead. Timing of the Christmas Eve sauna varies from family to family, but the trip to the cemetery is a tradition that everyone in Finland observes together.

The flag of Finland is flanked by candles as a window display. The flag is often incorporated into Christmas decorations.

Candles in the Cemetery

At sunset, Finnish people everywhere make their way to their local cemeteries to honor the dead in a simple yet strikingly beautiful ceremony that is at the very heart of Christmas in Finland.

Families place candles and sometimes wreaths on the graves of loved ones, lighting churchyards and cemeteries across the country with thousands of rows of little shining lights. Cemeteries often provide a special area for people whose loved ones are buried elsewhere so they, too, can light candles in remembrance this night. There is a brief service at 5 P.M. in many cemeteries. People may sing hymns or simply reflect quietly before heading home again.

In some places, children make special beeswax candles in school to place on the graves on Christmas Eve. In the past, people made the candles at home. According to folklore, you needed to

A Finnish cemetery is resplendent
with candles on the graves and
a large Christmas tree (above).
A family visits the grave of a loved
one, decorated with lanterns and
candles, on Christmas Eve (right).

have a happy frame of mind when casting the candles for them to
turn out right.

This cemetery ritual, like other parts of the Finnish Christmas
observance, has a connection to the ancient past. In pre-Christian
times, people believed that at the winter solstice the spirits of the
dead were present among the living. Food was left out on the
tables overnight on Christmas Eve and families slept in the straw on
the floor, so that the dead would have good things to eat and a cozy
place to rest when they returned to visit. Although these customs
are no longer practiced, the reverent attention to the dead remains.

The modern custom of placing candles on graves on Christmas
Eve began in the 1920's when candles were placed on the graves of
soldiers. After World War II, the visit to the cemetery became a
widespread tradition.

These days, special attention is given to honoring the war dead
on this night, with former soldiers marching in procession to local

cemeteries to pay tribute to their fallen comrades. In Helsinki, army officers are joined by representatives of various social organizations as they stand guard at the tomb of Marshal Mannerheim, the Finnish general who helped lead the country's fight for freedom and later served as the new country's president, first in 1918 and again in 1944.

The importance of this simple candle-lighting ceremony goes deep into the understanding of what it means to be Finnish.

The history of Finland is a difficult story of dominance, war, and finally independence. Again and again over the centuries, the country struggled against and was overtaken and ruled by its two powerful neighbors, Sweden and Russia. In 1917, the country finally gained true independence, only to suffer great hardship and loss of life during a 1918 civil war and later wars with Russia between 1939 and 1944. Each time the Finns have tasted bitter defeat or hardship, they have endured proudly.

The Finns have a word for it—*sisu*. Almost impossible to translate, sisu is at the heart of Finnish character. It is a personal quality of endurance against the odds, of surviving and staying true to what is meaningful. As the Finns stand silently in the cemeteries this Christmas Eve night, this quality brings strength and peace to many of their hearts.

> The importance of this simple candle-lighting ceremony goes deep into the understanding of what it means to be Finnish.

Home for Christmas Eve Dinner

You stomp the snow from your boots, shake off the cold, and come inside. A glass of something warm and spirited is needed to take off the chill after the snowy cemetery service. On Christmas Eve, a Finnish home is just the place to find wonderful, soul-warming drinks of all kinds.

At every Finnish Christmas celebration, spirits are warmed with mulled wine and homemade beer or near beer. *Sahti*, now the word for all home-brewed beers, originally was the name of a home-brewed nonalcoholic beer and much-loved Christmas drink in Finland.

Once every Finnish housewife knew how to brew beer. For Christmas, she would replace regular home-brewed beer with a special strong and hearty holiday drink. As part of the holiday tradition in a magic and myth-loving country, beer brewing soon took on magic of its own. Charms were spoken and good luck pieces were thrown into beer as it brewed. The housewife whose head was buzzing with chores of Christmas had better keep her spirit bright when brewing beer. One harsh word from her and the brew would be spoiled.

Christmas glögi, the Finnish adaptation of the Swedish Christmas drink glogg, has joined beer in recent years as a holiday favorite in Finland. A warm, spicy, fragrant wine drink, glögi is perfect for putting a warm glow back into the cheeks of those just in from the cold.

Glögi comes in many variations—using red or white wine, a port, or currant wine, and a range of spices. Cinnamon, ginger, cloves, and orange zest are traditional glögi spices, although Finnish cooks have found many ways to spice things up further. Delicious nonalcoholic versions are made using currant and other berry juices. Raisins and peeled almonds are provided, so that each partygoer can drop as many as he or she likes into a warm, spicy drink.

Everyone is warmed up and ready for the Finnish Christmas feast—a meal that is both rich and robust. Traditionally, the dinner centers around a baked ham and a variety of tasty vegetable casseroles, especially including rutabaga

Christmas glögi, or mulled wine, is accompanied by cookies (below). A beautiful array of traditional Christmas dishes awaits a crowd (bottom).

casserole and potato or carrot casserole, smoked whitefish and herring with sauces, salmon, lutefish, liver pate, fruit soup, fruit salad, breads and pastries, and rice or prune pudding.

In the Finnish Archipelago, the many scattered islands that lie in the Baltic Sea off Finland's west coast, Christmas dinner means *jouluhauki*—Christmas pike. The fisherman of Åland and the many islands close at hand know that pike fishing is at its best during the Christmas season, and the best food belongs on the Christmas table.

Traditionally, Christmas pike is prepared and served in a pot, surrounded by potatoes, rutabagas, and onions. Alongside is a horseradish sauce and maybe a chopped, hard-boiled egg. To the islanders, Christmas pike is a taste treat fit for a king—or a president. Each year, the fishermen of Korpoo present a prize Christmas pike to the president of Finland.

No Christmas dinner in Finland could end without *joulutortut*, Finnish Yuletide prune turnovers, or *piparkakut*, gingerbread cookies. The lovely aroma of

Children dressed in the traditional red Christmas gnome hats help their mother cut Christmas cookies into many shapes. Note the straw decorations in the background, especially the elaborate himmeli hanging near the window.

Gingerbread houses are part of Christmas in Finland. Here two young women (right) assemble and decorate the pieces they carefully cut out and baked (left). Note that they wear red Christmas gnome hats.

baking fills the home throughout the Christmas season. Along with the gingerbread houses and cookies, there will be *korvapuustit*—Finnish cinnamon buns, raisin cakes, an assortment of pastries, and *pulla*, the Finnish braided coffee bread.

Gingerbread–To Your Health!

Christmas and the spicy smell of gingerbread are inseparable in Finland. In olden times, the spices in gingerbread were considered helpful medicine. Allspice, for example, was used to treat listlessness and depression. In Germany, where gingerbread got its start, early gingerbread cookies were called "medicinal pancakes."

Today, anyone can tell you that tasty gingerbread cookies cut in holiday shapes and decorated with icing work wonders when it comes to feeling warm and good inside on a cold, dark December day.

Gingerbread house building is a happy Christmas pastime in Finland. Houses, churches, and castles are created by little and big hands alike. Finnish architects have even been known to take the gingerbread challenge in competitions of their own.

Rice Porridge for Elves and Everyone

There is a special treat yet to come—rice porridge. Once a central dish in Christmas dinner itself, rice porridge is now likely to be eaten first thing Christmas Eve morning or as a late afternoon or evening snack, either in a little meal all its own or with raisin soup on the side.

Family members wear their red Christmas gnome hats as they participate in the old custom of sharing rice porridge at Christmas.

Rice, when it first arrived with traders from the Far East, was a rare and treasured treat in Finland. In past times and in hard times, rice porridge sometimes might be really more of a pudding with only a few token grains of hard-to-get rice in each serving. In the hardest of times, there was only "snowflake soup," the raisin soup with a few "snowflakes" of rice floating in the bowl.

In good times or bad, rice porridge is always more than meets the eye. Your serving may contain a surprise. By ancient custom, one almond is mixed into the Christmas porridge. If it turns up in your bowl, you will be lucky in the year ahead. You may not feel so lucky this evening, though, because the almond also bestows an obligation. The almond bearer must rise to entertain the others or may be assigned a job for the day to earn his or her good fortune.

Rice porridge has been a favorite of Finnish elves for centuries. On Christmas Eve, porridge was set out in barns and stables and the family sauna to please the guardian elves living there. To please your house elf, prepare a little extra porridge for his Christmas treat. A satisfied elf is likely to stick around and protect you from troubles in the year ahead.

A Visit from Joulupukki

On Christmas Eve around the world, parents remind their little ones that Santa Claus won't come until they are fast asleep, that no one—except maybe the family cat—will see old St. Nick drop down the chimney and go straight to his work.

Not so in Finland. Before setting off on his whirlwind world tour, Santa—Joulupukki to the children of Finland—makes a personal visit to each and every child in his home country. As afternoon becomes evening on the day before Christmas, Finnish children wait for Santa Claus—looking a lot like an uncle or family friend under that red suit—to come right through the front door bringing presents for all.

Little children often wait dressed in red felt hats and gray and red elf suits. After all, they will serve as Santa's helper elves when there are presents to distribute.

Suddenly, Joulupukki is here! He asks his all-important question, "Are there any good children here?" He hears a hearty "YES!" in reply and opens his sack of surprises. Joulupukki dresses and acts just like Santa Claus—he is Santa Claus, in fact. But his Finnish name translates as "Yule Buck."

In pagan times, the holiday season surrounding the winter solstice was a time to ward off evil spirits and hope for good in the coming new year. Finnish families were visited on one special night in the darkest days of winter by a gruff goat—the original Joulupukki. This far-from-jolly visitor, represented by a real goat or a neighbor draped in animal skins, menaced and scolded everyone he saw. And he didn't give presents; he demanded them. Adults were quick to shower food and gifts on their nasty guest, and children promised to be good in hope that the goat would assure health and a bountiful harvest in the year ahead.

Over time, the old goat caught the spirit of giving. Still, he stomped around and threatened the children, questioning their behavior. Once satisfied that there were good children in the home,

Joulupukki arrives on Christmas Eve for a group of children dressed as his helpers.

he threw presents on the floor. As generations passed, the holiday visitor grew more jolly than gruff. There was only a quick goodness quiz for the children, then presents tossed in through the door.

In Finland, Christmas was once called *nakkovaika*, which translates as "throw time," because of the goat's graceless delivery style. The gifts still are sometimes called *joulukolkutus*, or Christmas knock, for the knock on the door when the gifts are left there.

Santa Claus, complete with red suit and kind disposition, first visited a few upper-class Finnish families in the 1800's. As word spread about his legendary generosity and Christmas cheer, Santa was invited into more and more Finnish homes.

Thanks in part to "Uncle Markus," a popular Finnish radio personality who revealed the whereabouts of Santa's Lapland home in a 1927 broadcast, the Joulupukki who comes around on Christmas Eve these days is every bit the Santa Claus of the red suit and reindeer.

Living in Lapland, surrounded by familiar Finnish elves and reindeer, the most famous jolly old elf in the world had no trouble taking the holiday duties away from a surly goat. Santa's Finnish name is still Joulupukki. He still asks "Are there any good children in this house?" But he always hears a yes, and there is nothing menacing about his "Ho, Ho, Ho!"

Finns exchange Christmas cards, too. This old example shows Joulupukki accompanied by a goat bearing gifts. The goat recalls the ancient origin of Joulupukki as a mean goat.

Joulupukki gives his new-found elves presents to pass out. Then he may have a warming drink or a gingerbread cookie and share a song or two with the children. Soon, however, he must hurry away to other houses on his busy route.

Santa's employment of elves made him seem as Finnish as could be from the start. Elves—and other little magical beings of the forest—were a mainstay of Finnish folklore long before Santa was discovered living in Lapland. Besides making toys in Santa's workshop, Santa's elves are said to spy on children—naughty and nice—all year long. In the past, each house was said to have its own protecting elf. You needed to be nice to the elf and make good food for him or he might leave and take your good luck away.

Rest and Relaxation on Christmas Day

Christmas Eve is packed with cherished traditions, family and friends, sauna, Santa, presents, and so much lovely food and drink. Christmas Day follows as a welcome day of quiet rest. Church services begin as early as 6 A.M. in some places. Still, churches everywhere are crowded with people who come to sing the much-loved carols and hymns and to welcome Christmas.

Then it's home to family, rest, and relaxation for the day. In the islands of the Finnish Archipelago, Christmas morning is time for raisin buns and whimsical rolls shaped like little people. Everywhere in Finland, warm and delicious breads, rolls, and pastries join the morning coffee. Later, there are terrific leftovers from the Christmas Eve feast to satisfy anyone still hungry. On this peaceful day, not a person is stirring except for little trips to the kitchen.

Christmas church services are held throughout Finland (below).

The city of Porvoo is blanketed with snow on a bluish December day. Porvoo has been an official town since 1346, but it was an important trading center even before that.

Steamy Christmas to All!

A Finnish family enjoys their traditional Christmas sauna together. The father holds a *vihta*, or bunch of birch twigs used to stimulate circulation.

It's 190 °F inside and so STEAMY. You're stripped down to nothing, dripping with sweat. From time to time, you grab a switch of birch twigs and swat your bare skin. Ahh! It's beginning to feel a lot like Christmas in Finland.

You might not decorate a tree one year or you might forego Grandma's rutabaga casserole recipe. Maybe the presents don't all get wrapped, or your family can't get away to celebrate at the lakeside cottage. Still, it will be Christmas—unless you skip the sauna.

There is no tradition as truly Finnish as the sauna. It is estimated that there are 1.5 million saunas in this country of fewer than 5 million people. A sauna can be found by nearly every dwelling from the elegant old painted wooden houses of Rauma to the glistening modern apartment buildings of Helsinki, to hotels, lake-

land cottages, and the simplest hut in the far reaches of Lapland.

Around the world, people have copied the Finns by building saunas so they too can enjoy the invigorating pleasure of a steam clean. In Finland, people know the sauna offers much more than that.

Finnish settlers built their sauna first to live in and sweat in while building a barn and finally a house. Finnish soldiers serving as United Nations peacekeeping troops are known for constructing saunas as a first order of business wherever they are sent, even if the destination is a hot, desert country.

Until present generations, the sauna was considered the proper place for childbirth. The dead were washed and prepared for burial there. Today, business deals are negotiated and political bargains struck on wooden sauna benches.

The sauna is the true spiritual center of the home. And it is central to the celebration of Christmas. In the steam heat of the sauna, Finnish people find both physical and spiritual rejuvenation. The sauna, protected by its own special elf, is considered a place of deep peace, especially at Christmas. Here, Finnish families meet to experience together a warm feeling of total well-being and to enter the religious and family-centered holiday in a renewed and prepared state.

In the past, people talked about "attending" the sauna on Christmas Eve. Today, the *joulusauna*—Christmas sauna—continues to be the holiday's one real requirement, and it is estimated that 70 percent of all Finns will have a sauna this night. Traveling about Finland on

al aromatic sauna with a real wood fire is still thought to produce the best *löyly*, or steamy sauna atmosphere.

The temperature in a sauna should be between 170-212 °F (80-100 °C). Participants sit in the hot steam for 15 to 30 minutes, with cool-offs in the changing room, or maybe a dip through a hole in a frozen lake or a quick roll in the snow. While steaming, Finns beat their bodies lightly with a *vihta*, a little whisk of birch twigs, to stimulate blood circulation.

In olden times, people believed that even the dead would have a sauna on this special night. Even today, the last person to use the sauna on Christmas Eve is sure to leave a good steam going for them.

When you enjoy a sauna on Christmas Eve is up to you. The Finnish will tell you it is best not to sauna after too much food and drink, so the late afternoon before the evening Christmas feast is when most people attend the sauna.

It is certain that everyone in the family will be finished with the sauna before midnight. Finnish folklore has it that the Devil himself shows up for a sauna at the stroke of 12 on Christmas Eve.

Christmas Eve, Santa can expect to see Christmas lights twinkling on downtown streets, candles burning in the windows of homes, and smoke rising from sauna chimneys everywhere.

The tradition of the Finnish sauna is over 2,000 years old. From ancient times, a sauna has been created by using a wood fire to heat a pile of stones in an enclosure. Water thrown on the stones produced the steam. Today, many saunas are electrically heated, but the tradition-

This old sauna hut in a Finnish forest is still in use, as you can see from the people on its porch (top). How about taking a dip in a frozen lake? The surface ice of this lake has been cut to allow a spot for this family to do just that (bottom).

In Lapland,
Santa feeds one
of his reindeer.

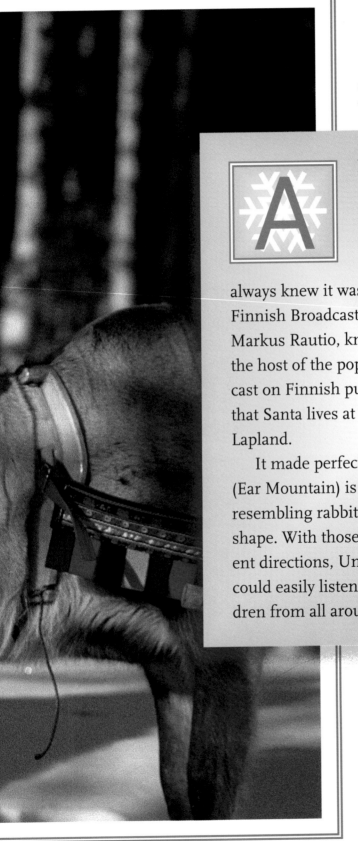

Lapland–Home to Santa Claus

All those reindeer, so much snow, those magical Northern Lights, the deep, inviting woods. . .Could he be nearby?

In their hearts, they always knew it was true. Then, in 1927, the Finnish Broadcasting Company made it official. Markus Rautio, known as "Uncle Markus," and the host of the popular "Children's Hour" broadcast on Finnish public radio, revealed on the air that Santa lives at Korvatunturi Fell in eastern Lapland.

It made perfect sense. Korvatunturi Fell (Ear Mountain) is named for the three peaks resembling rabbit ears that create its distinctive shape. With those magical ears tuned to different directions, Uncle Markus explained, Santa could easily listen for the wishes of good children from all around the world.

As the international borderline of Lapland and Russia runs along its peak, Korvatunturi is in a zone that is off-limits to travel. From his Lapland mountain, Santa can enjoy the snowy landscape he loves, and his privacy is assured. Never one to disappoint children of any age, Santa welcomes the public to his nearby workshop and post office all year round, however.

At Home with Santa

Care to visit the jolly old elf? You first arrive in Rovaniemi, the capital of Lapland. It is a modern city serving 57,000, of whom 35,000 live within the city limits. It sits just inside the Arctic Circle and is the largest city that far north.

Rovaniemi is a great place to witness the unstoppable spirit of the Finnish people. The first major city established in northern Finland, Rovaniemi was originally a trading post and provision center for those headed into the wilds of the Arctic. Completely destroyed in the fierce fighting of World War II, Rovaniemi was quickly rebuilt, and it was rebuilt in style. The city plan and several of its prominent buildings were designed by famed Finnish architect Alvar Aalto. In practical yet playful style, the streets of the city are laid out to resemble a reindeer's antlers.

Santa checks his lists as he sits outside the entrance to Santa Park in Lapland.

Santa Claus Land, as Laplanders call the region where Santa can be found 364 days a year, is only a short drive—or sleigh ride or snowmobile run—from Rovaniemi and its international airport. Together Finnair and the Finnish Tourist Board have kept the Rovaniemi airport busy.

Each year over 40,000 children and adults arrive from other countries to see the wonders of Santa's northern home and experience a little Finnish Christmas fun. At Christmastime, over 100 charter flights arrive in Lapland's principal airport from Great Britain alone. Children from Japan and the United States also top the list of Lapland visitors.

Santa waves from the entrance of his private plane, decorated with his picture.

Santa himself has taken to modern air travel on all but one night of the year. Giving the reindeer a rest, he flies his own signature planes to visit countries around the world and personally extend his welcome to Finland. Since the 1980's, Finnair has proudly proclaimed itself the "Official Carrier for Santa Claus." It provides Santa with his own plane bearing a large illustration of Santa and his sleigh on its side.

When it comes to children in need of special cheering, Santa's welcome is warm indeed. Working with Finnair and the Finnish Tourist Board, Santa has accompanied groups of sick children from as far away as Japan and the United States to visit Lapland, see his workshop, enjoy reindeer rides and sleighing, and have all kinds of other winter holiday fun as his personal guests.

One Very Cozy Post Office

Touring Santa's world, your likely first stop will be Santa's Main Post Office, located in Santa's Workshop Village at Napapiiri, just outside Rovaniemi. Arriving at Santa's Village by sleigh or shuttle is like stepping into a page from a lovely Christmas storybook. Nestled into the snowy woods you'll find a collection of charming log cabin buildings.

Inside, a cheerful crowd of Santa's helpers are sorting mail, seeing to packages, and filling requests for their international visitors. The "elves" speak a number of languages and are happy to accept parcels and letters anytime of year for delivery at Christmas. To keep current with Santa's lengthy list of good children, the workshop elves have gone high-tech. In the workshop, you'll see them busy at their computer keyboards. You may even find them chatting on the World Wide Web (see address in Dear Santa sidebar on pages 46-47).

At Santa's main post office, you'll discover a beautiful display of highly prized Finland Christmas stamps. Each year, a prominent Finnish artist is honored with the coveted task of depicting Christmas in Finland in a tiny stamp scene. Since the tradition began in 1973, these stamps have been treasured by children and collectors around the world.

In addition, the post office sells beautiful Lapland postcards, souvenirs, toys, books, and Christmas decorations. Santa's elves themselves often are delightfully represented on Finnish Christmas cards.

Santa's Village in Lapland is gaily lit in the bluish December light.

Anything sent from Santa's main post office is stamped with that one-of-a-kind Arctic Circle postmark. Every visitor also receives an official certificate as proof of his or her visit. Hang on to it. After all, who is going to believe you actually saw Santa's workshop?

Santa's complex of post office and workshops all grew from one tiny, charming cabin built in 1950 to accommodate America's former first lady, Eleanor Roosevelt. She was intrigued by Lapland and requested a visit. Whether Mrs. Roosevelt, a first lady but also a mother and grandmother, had a secret conference with Santa on her trip is not known. We do know that she was captivated on her visit by Lapland itself and by the friendly people living there.

When children around the world learned that Santa's home had been discovered on Korvatunturi, letters to Santa began pouring in to Lapland. Santa's village was constructed and, in 1996, opened to the public. The village is open all year long with extended hours during the month of December.

Can't visit in person? Send Santa a letter. He loves to get mail. Or send him an e-mail. See pages 46-47 for instructions.

SantaPark: Santa's Year-Round Party

He's world-famous for his happy extravagance when it comes to pleasing children on one special day. Now Santa has opened his very own theme park near his Arctic Circle home so he can delight children and adults all year around. The brand new

Inside the cave of the mountain at Santa Park are a carousel and other entertainment (below). The entrance to the park in the cave is bright against the snowy landscape of the mountain (bottom).

Children and adults enjoy riding the carousel in the cave at SantaPark.

SantaPark is located in the Arctic Circle just outside Rovaniemi.

A theme park in the Arctic Circle? Isn't it a little cold? No problem for Santa! He built Santa-Park deep inside a mountain. Sounds fantastic, and it is. And this is no ordinary park packed with hectic, loud, dizzying rides. Santa's park is a place of pure magic, Santa style.

From nearby Santa Claus Village, a shuttle takes guests on the short trip to SantaPark. Or you can travel there in a sleigh drawn by reindeer, ride a sled pulled by huskies, or ride on a snowmobile.

Your destination is Syvävaara Fell, the mountain that contains the park. Deep inside the mountain is a huge cavern holding the park center with a beautiful Christmas carousel and all sorts of Christmas fun. From here, you can follow four corridors out to a surrounding hall filled with attractions and rides.

Take the Magic Sleigh Ride, which transports you through the wonders of Lapland in every season from deep winter snow to sunlit midsummer nights. There are puppet shows, reindeer rides, climbing adventures, shops, games, and a Countdown Clock ticking off the days and minutes to Christmas. Ride Santa's helicopters and check out his workshop in action or watch a multimedia show complete with northern lights. And, of course, you'll see reindeer and maybe even meet Santa himself.

SantaPark is built to accommodate 1,000 visitors at a time. In its first few weeks of operations during Christmas 1998, for example, the park welcomed over 40,000 visitors. This theme park is the newest and most elaborate attraction to welcome people from around the world to enjoy Santa's snowy homeland.

Romp with Rudolph

Want to join in reindeer games? Your next stop on the Lapland Christmas tour should be Salla Reindeer Park, to the east of Rovaniemi, outside the town of Salla itself. This large national preserve is open all year around to offer Finns and adventurers from

around the world a look at life in a reindeer herders' settlement and a taste of life in the wild.

At Salla Reindeer Park, children and adults can take a reindeer sleigh ride and even earn their own reindeer driving licenses. A crash course in the what, how, where, and why of reindeers is offered, plus a look at reindeer predators such as the wolf, wolverine, and golden eagle.

Children are able to pet and feed tame reindeer in the park and learn how to throw a Lappish lasso. They also can go on husky sled safaris, try ice fishing, watch reindeer races, and otherwise live like real Lapland reindeer herders for a day.

During the Christmas season, Salla Reindeer Park offers snowshoe treks and snowmobile rides through the wilderness, and overnight stays in a log cabin. In a Lapp hut, visitors drink coffee from a traditional black pot and eat Lappish cake and salmon.

Reindeer in Lapland herd together (top). Reindeer are useful animals for the Lapps. Here they pull sleighs full of visitors (bottom).

Dear Santa

etters arrive at Santa Claus's Main Post Office in Lapland from children all over the world. Santa loves to receive—and send—mail. Wish lists and queries and thank-you notes come in from Great Britain, Japan, Poland, India, the United States, Brazil, and everywhere else. Each year, Santa answers hundreds of thousands of letters from children. Would someone on your list like a letter from Santa?

For about 6 dollars (30 Finnish markkas), you can write to Santa, and he will send a personal letter in any of 12 languages to you or your special little someone. Each year Santa creates a new letter, complete with humorous

A Finnish Christmas stamp is designed every year to be used on Santa's mail (below).

A group of Santa's Christmas gnomes uses modern technology to help Santa answer the thousands of letters he gets each year at his post office in Lapland (bottom).

illustrations, on his own private stationery. Along with his personal message, Santa encloses a little gift for every child. If you like, Santa's letter also will include a postscript hinting at an adult's involvement in the surprise. The envelope features a beautiful Finnish Christmas stamp franked at Santa's own post office. Write to Santa at

Santa Claus's Main Post Office
Arctic Circle
Finland

Below is an example of the kind of answer children receive from Santa Claus in response to a letter to the Santa Claus Post Office.

Or reach Santa's Main Post Office quickly on the World Wide Web at http://www.santaclaus.posti.fi.

Other fun Finnish Santa sites to visit are:

Santa's Official Fan Club (http://www.santaclausoffice.fi)

Here you can join the club and receive stories, games and news from Santa, an Advent calendar, and a birthday card

The Official Santa Claus Radio Station (http://www.nettiradio.fi)

Here you can read or listen to Christmas stories and hear a daily greeting from Santa himself.

Santa Claus Main Post Office
at Christmas 1998

...re waiting for Christmas as much as I am! I looked at my diary
...n good this year also. That's great!
...you so that waiting for Christmas won't seem so long.
...old in Lapland. Snowdrifts are piled high and it's freezing
...ting my toy workshop, and while writing this I'm sipping

...ryone is scampering about because it's getting so close to
...helpers are busy day and night. Today the woodshop gnomes
...r and even got to try them. Anni, the gnome from the book
...colourful books to the gift wrapping department. Would your
...did you even ask for a book? I'll have to check.
...p, the gnomes are busying themselves with the computer games.
...out them. I'd rather play battleship with my cat. You don't

...l of letters just came in the mail. I'll read them in the afternoon.
...e stable told me that the reindeer were restless in the
...little scared from last night's amazing Northern Lights.
...al storms in the sky and sometime they are so powerful
...the workshops. Luckily the Northern Lights don't
...en socks...

...keeper gnome just came into the office and we have
...her. But in the evening I'll go to the sauna, like
...and that will be fun!

Santa Claus

...mber to remind you to send
...ur friends, especially to

Finns enjoy a snowy picnic on St. Stephen's Day, December 26.

A Winter Wonderland

hristmas Day provided a quiet rest. One day later, everyone is up and out the door for fun in the snow and on the ice. December 26, Boxing Day in many countries, is *tapaninpäivä*—St. Stephen's Day—in Finland. This holiday signals the beginning of a long playful break in this winter wonderland. With children out of school and many adults on vacation, Finns can be found at their island or lakeland cottages, on husky or snowmobile safaris, cruising the arctic waters, trekking or skiing forest paths, playing every winter sport—even ice surfing and ice golf! They're out, and out for fun.

Traditionally, St. Stephen's Day was the time for a holiday sleigh ride to visit relatives. Such a pleasant custom is hard to let go, and today social clubs and holiday resorts organize sleigh rides on this day.

Rides in the snow are the order of the day, on traditional sleds, kick sleds (like scooters without wheels), and especially spinning boom sleds. To devise a bit of traditional holiday fun for their children, Finns make a spinning boom sled by drilling a hole in a frozen lake, then freezing an axle post in the hole. Next, a long, sturdy pole is fixed to the axle, and a sled is attached to the far end of the pole. By pushing the pole in a circle around the axle, adults can provide their little ones with a wild, homemade carousel ride.

Children enjoy a ride on a boom sled atop frozen ground (above). Snowmobiling is a method of transportation as well as a popular sport in Finland (below).

Hit the Trails

In Lapland, the snowmobile is the standard mode of transportation for going from place to place, herding reindeer, and getting things done. At holiday time, the snowmobile reclaims its sporty image.

The Finnish National Board of Forestry maintains over 3,700 miles of snowmobile tracks through the wilderness. You can jump on a trail in the heart of Rovaniemi and head out for days of adventure, stopping at campsites or in cabins along the route to eat and sleep.

Cross-country skiing is done all over Finland. This skiier is in Lapland.

A family enjoys entertainment and food in one of the huts scattered across Lapland.

Others set out on foot or on skis to work off holiday meals in the fresh, open air or explore the woods.

Snowmobilers, hikers, and skiers traveling the wilderness can count on the kindness of strangers for a safe, warm place to stop and rest. All across Lapland, a network of more than 200 huts provide shelter to anyone who needs it. Some are private and must be reserved in advance, but most are free and unlocked. A hut is available to every person who stops there until it is full each night.

Huts have bunks, cooking facilities, a pile of dry firewood, maybe some dry food, and sometimes even a wilderness telephone. Some huts even include a sauna. The "wilderness rule" is that the last person to arrive at a hut will be given the best place to sleep. In other words, stay only one night and be ready to give up your spot to an arriving weary traveler.

Try Something Different

In Finland, as elsewhere, the Christmas season is also a time to get away from the ordinary. It is common for Finns in the city to have a summer home elsewhere and very common to find them celebrating Christmas there. After all, what could be more Christmasy than a cabin in the woods?

Popular getaway areas include the Lakeland region and the many tiny islands of Finland's Archipelago. On Åland, the largest of the islands in the Baltic Sea, Finns enjoy skating on the frozen bays during Christmas or dropping a line through a hole in the ice and "jigging" for fish.

All through the Christmas holiday season, Finns take to the sea to celebrate. From mid-November until after New Year's, Finland's two largest ferry lines, Silja and Viking, are packed with holiday revelers. On board, people escape to Christmas, Finland style. The ship's buffets are packed with delicious traditional Christmas fare, and Christmas programs for children are provided.

People fly into Finland from all over the world at Christmas for the once-in-a-lifetime experience of an icebreaker cruise. The Sampo, the world's only recreational icebreaker, sails from the Finnish port of Kemi in the northern Gulf of Bothnia.

The ship cuts through thin surface ice without a sound. Encountering pack ice, it charges ahead, crashing and pounding its way. Out in the open sea, the ship will stop, and passengers can choose to climb out and actually stand on the frozen surface of the

Cruise passengers enjoy a dip in a swimming hole their ship has cut through the ice for them. The swimmers wear protective clothing especially designed for this purpose.

A Finnish family enjoys a visit to an ice house glowing from candlelight and decorated with pine boughs.

sea or, wearing protective gear, take a swim in the hole the ship has cut in the ice.

Back on board, the adventurers enjoy a warming buffet of Finnish Christmas food and drink.

For those who want to live for a while in the snowy world of Christmas and reindeer, Lapland offers a variety of fun places to stay. Finns and foreign travelers alike book Christmas lodging in northern cabins, Sami huts, even igloos made of ice.

At Ranua Zoo, children play with lynx cubs.

A Holiday for Animals

Animals are included in the Christmas fun in Finland. Besides leaving special sheaves of grain out for the birds, Finns are sure to treat all animals, both domestic and wild, kindly at Christmas.

In past times, horses were even invited to sample the prize Christmas brew. Because St. Stephen himself was said to be King Herod's stableman, it seemed only right to feast with the horses on St. Stephen's special day. Men would eat and drink in the stable and pour beer on the horses' hay. Afterwards, horses were

A sturdy Finnish horse pulls a sleigh full of visitors.

hitched to sleighs and both men and beasts worked off their heavy meal in a wild race through the countryside.

Today horses enjoy a more peaceful celebration. They are given oats and a sampling of the family's Christmas bread. Some people decorate their stables with evergreens during the holidays, and here and there a young rider will treat his or her horse to the last pieces of gingerbread when Christmas is coming to a close.

Ranua Zoo near Rovaniemi is the northernmost zoo in the world. The native snow-loving animals of Ranua party daily during the Christmas holidays with children who visit from around the world to see lynx, moose, wolverines, wolves, and other arctic species in their natural habitat. Like all Finns, the tame lynxes of this arctic zoo are at their happiest hosting many Little Christmas parties for their guests. They love to be petted and pose with children for a holiday photo.

Traditions of the Sami

The region of Lapland includes the far northern parts of Finland, Norway, Sweden, and Russia. Finland's snowy province of Lapland, comprising nearly half the country, is one of the last great wilderness areas of Europe. And it is the arctic home of the Sami, a nomadic, reindeer-herding people who have inhabited Finland for over 6,000 years.

Existing in a world alive with wildlife and natural beauty but veiled in darkness and cold for months each winter, the ancient Sami developed a complex spiritual relationship with their surroundings. Natural wonders—lakes, rock formations—were imbued with sacred meaning. Sami folklore also was filled with witches and magical beings possessing amazing powers.

The winter solstice—the moment during the deepest days of winter when the shortest day occurs and the Earth begins its travels back to days filled with light—has always been a special time of magic and meaning for Finland's Sami people. The powers of the spirit world—witches and the like—seemed especially strong at this dark time of year. In response, many Sami customs were devised for keeping peace on Earth and fostering good will among people.

For thousands of years, the Sami had followed their reindeer herds all across their far north region. When the Finns arrived, the nomadic Sami people were pushed farther and farther north to their present-day home of Lapland. In the 1600's, the dominant Finns, suspicious of the Sami's magical culture, forced them to convert to Christianity. The Sami's cult sites, their witch drums, and other religious objects were destroyed. Still, the ancient culture couldn't be driven from their hearts.

Adopting Christmas as the central winter holiday, the Sami brought their own ideas to its celebration. Like the Finns, the Sami store up the best foods for Christmas dinner. In the north country, this means the fattest salmon, reindeer milk, and cheese.

A Sami reindeer herder rounds up a traditional mode of transportation with a modern one—a snowmobile (top left). Here a Sami man leads one of his working reindeer pulling an empty sled (right).

Still, it is hard to focus on the food during the Christmas season. Dangerous, magical beings are said to be in the air and everywhere—and they must be appeased. As Christmas Eve approaches, all work must be finished, firewood chopped, everything made right. Even the ground outside the cone-shaped *kota* (the traditional Sami dwelling) must be smooth and clear.

This night, it is said, the unseen are out and about, racing wildly all over Lapland on sleds pulled by reindeer, dogs, bulls, rabbits, squirrels—even mice. They are up to every kind of strange behavior, holding weddings and trading things, and they want no interference from people. Should a sled bump over a twig near a kota, the riders might rain down disaster on the family inside. If they became thirsty, they might stop and drink your blood.

Things don't ease up much the next day, either. According to custom, all work and play must stop during the Christmas season. Staalu, the witch of Lapland, is likely to grab and eat any children found out sledding now.

Over time, the joy of Christmas overtook the darkness of the season. The Sami began to put up Christmas trees or, above the arctic border, whatever they could fashion to resemble a Christmas tree. Staalu, taking her cue from her Finnish neighbor Joulupukki, began pulling presents out of her bag instead of stuffing children in.

Fasting is no longer required on Christmas Eve. Roast reindeer may now appear in the Christmas Eve feast, along with grouse or other native wild game. There is fish, of course, plus Finnish vegetable casseroles. The berries of Lapland—lingonberries, arctic bramble berries, and delicate cloudberries—help sweeten things up.

A roaring fire warms a welcoming traditional Sami hut, known as a kota.

And there is traditional porridge with a hidden almond. In some places, a lucky Laplander may find a small bone from a reindeer's rear hoof, rather than an almond, in his or her bowl.

An extra bowl of porridge will be poured in Lapland this night, not for elves, but for Staalu herself. Other spirits may stop by, too, but they behave in a more playful and less threatening manner these days. Maybe it helps that the meat and pastries from Christmas Eve dinner are left out overnight for them.

Today, the Sami people, their arctic skills, cultural traditions, language, and art are seen as a treasured part of Finland's past—and its future. At the Arktikum museum in the Lapp capital of Rovaniemi, Sami witch drums and other artifacts that escaped destruction by invading cultures are being studied and recreated as the people of Finland strive to enhance understanding of this complex culture and respect for the Sami.

Many people gather for the traditional outdoor New Year's celebration in Helsinki.

New Year's Fun and Fortune

 ew Year's Eve arrives in Finland bringing with it another holiday feast, plus some special magic all its own. Delicious holiday casseroles, hams, pastries, and drinks are offered in plenty as friends and family gather at home for spirited fun. Other families head out to join a citywide New Year's Eve celebration.

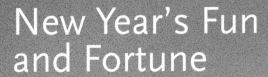

Looking into the Future

In Finnish homes, the magic of playful folklore casts a warm glow on this special night. Tradition holds that New Year's Eve is the perfect time for fortune-telling, and Finns everywhere have fun while casting for news of their futures this night.

According to an ancient Finnish custom, a piece of melted tin can tell what shape your future will take. A little tin is melted over the New Year's fire, then quickly cast into a bucket of cold water. When cooled, the tin piece is held up near a wall. The shadow of its new shape predicts your coming year.

For many years, Finns have celebrated New Year's with fortunes "told" from shapes of melted tin (top). Children dip the melted tin into water to cool and harden it (below).

Is it shaped like a bird? You're in for a high-flying year. Shaped like a boat, plane, or car? Travel is in store. Just a wadded, crinkly mess? Don't despair. That's a wad of money coming your way!

The water used to cool the tin is reserved, for it holds magic of its own. Place a handkerchief dipped in the water under your pillow this night and you will see your future spouse in a dream.

The custom of telling fortunes in melted tin has ancient roots, arriving in Scandinavia from central Europe hundreds of years ago. Finnish families "cast" fortunes at New Year's parties in the 1700's, and they have been seeing their shadows every New Year's Eve since.

Maybe a coffee cup holds news for you. Another popular Finnish New Year's game suggests it is so. Called "Lifting the Mankara," this fortune-telling party game is played by hiding a selection of meaningful items under overturned coffee cups. Mankara means "tiny doll," one of the objects you might find.

Each person takes a turn selecting two or more cups to turn over. The discovered items predict various aspects of their future. For the next turn, all the items are returned, the cups are mixed up, and it's time for someone else to choose.

What's there to find? Traditional surprises include a coin—meaning wealth or a windfall; red yarn—a happy new year; black yarn—grief in the new year; a ring—marriage; a sugar cube—a sweet life; a bit of bread—life continuing just as it is now; a pin—the "prick" of illness or misfortune to come; a key—a new home; a little yarn doll—a new baby. To this standard list of items, families often add or substitute a few ideas of their own to give special meaning or humor to the game.

Find a ring? Wonder who your spouse will be? An old Finnish New Year's game played with mirrors might give you a glimpse. The reflection of one mirror placed against a black shawl and surrounded by candles is caught and reflected back and forth with another facing mirror. At the stroke of midnight on New Year's Eve, the image of a future spouse was said to walk in the reflections. Unfortunately, a coffin—a truly bad omen—might be seen there instead.

Here a ladleful of melted tin is poured into a bucket of water (top). A wad of melted, hardened tin waits for its shape to be "read" as someone's fortune (bottom).

Finns everywhere
celebrate New Year's
with fireworks.

City Celebrations

In cities across Finland, the bright lights and Christmas decorations seem to shine even brighter tonight as the new year approaches. Everywhere, Finns leave their homes late in the evening to crowd the downtown streets and celebrate the final hour of the old year and see in the new with friends and strangers alike.

Helsinki hosts a national New Year's party in its Senaatintori Square. Shown on television across the country, the Helsinki event offers festive holiday music, a speech by the mayor of Helsinki, and an address by a priest from the Lutheran Cathedral. Fireworks boom as the bells of the cathedral toll out the last moments of the old year.

In Turku, the New Year's celebration will be held on the stairs of the 700-year-old Turku Cathedral, regarded as the national shrine and mother church of the Evangelical Lutheran Church of Finland. Fireworks follow on Samppalinna Hill.

In small town squares and around civic Christmas trees all over Finland, the scene is repeated. People gather to listen to speeches by mayors and other civic leaders and wait for church bells to ring out the old year and ring in the new. Churches offer

New Year's services with hymns and prayers for peace in the year to come. The new year arrives in Finland to merry toasting and shouting, a rousing rendition of the national anthem, and fireworks both public and private.

Like Christmas Day, New Year's Day itself is a day of rest for everyone. A long night of play and partying leads to a day of quiet and homebound relaxation. At noon, most Finns will turn on the television to watch as Finland's president gives his New Year's address. Otherwise, not a creature is stirring once again.

Nuuttipukki Makes His Rounds

The Christmas season comes to a close with *loppiainen*, or Epiphany, on January 6. This is the day most Finnish families take down the tree and pack up decorations for next year. Still, one more group of Christmas visitors is expected. According to old Finnish custom, St. Canute's Day, January 19, was the day *nuuttipukit*, or Canute goats, came calling.

In the past, just as the Christmas straw was being cleared from under the table, there was a knock and nuuttipukit appeared at the door asking for that last drop or two of the hearty Christmas brew. The thirsty goats were neighbors and friends wearing their coats inside out and a goat's mask or horns and bearing a sheaf of straw. They sang for their beer and usually were welcomed in to enjoy a last holiday party and finish off the brew.

These party-loving, playful fellows were clearly distant relatives of Joulupukki. The straw Christmas goats standing in front of Finnish houses and hanging from Finnish Christmas tree branches today celebrate all the happy goats of the long and merry season.

In Turku, Turku Cathedral is where the local New Year's celebration is centered.

The Northern Lights

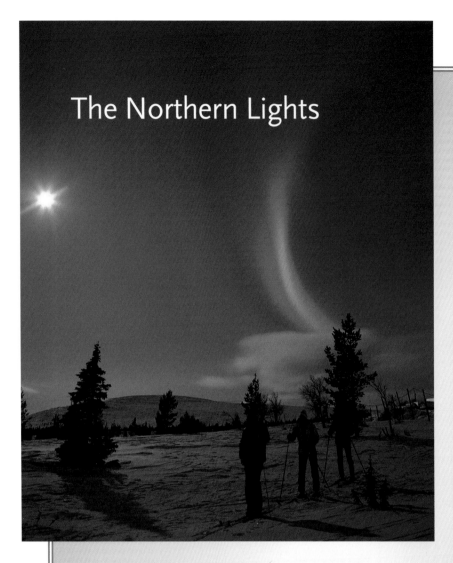

The moving northern lights constantly change as they appear in the dark sky.

Northern lights can come in any weather, any time of year, but somehow they seem to fit perfectly with the long dark nights and bright, colorful lights of the Christmas season. After all, what better place to see the northern lights, or aurora borealis, than standing outside in the snow on a Christmas night above the Arctic Circle in Finland?

hat causes those gigantic streaks, waves, and swirls of green, red, and white to pulse and dance across the icy, dark winter sky?

Scientists say the northern lights occur when wind from the sun throws electrically charged particles into contact with Earth's atmosphere. Ancient Sami folklore attributes the light show to a legendary fox spirit who whisks his tail around, throwing colorful snowflakes about in the sky.

Both ideas sound fantastic, but it takes a fantastic idea to explain the wonder of the northern lights as seen from a snowy cabin in Lapland in the dark of a Christmas season night.

When should you stand outside? Predicting just when the sun—or a legendary fox—will act up can be tricky. Therefore, many Lapland hotels employ northern light sentinels, people who promise to watch and wake up interested guests should the lights put on a show in the middle of the night.

You can be sure to catch the northern lights all year around and even at midday at the Arctic Research Center housed in the Arktikum in Rovaniemi, Lapland. Here, the Finnish Meteorological Board stages a light show of its own, complete with a primer on how and why.

Finnish Crafts

Star Boy Hat

You Will Need

White poster board, 26" x 15"

Pencil

String

Scissors

Glue

Gold and silver glitter

Stapler

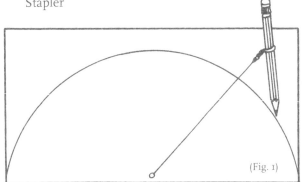

(Fig. 1)

What to Do

1. Mark a point halfway (13") across the bottom edge of the 26" board. With a piece of string tied around a pencil, hold the string taught at the center point so the pencil just reaches the edge of the paper. Draw a half circle, which should have a diameter of 26" (Fig. 1).

2. Cut out the half circle. With a bottle of glue, draw stars on it (Fig. 2). Then sprinkle gold and silver glitter on the glue. Carefully shake off the excess. Allow glue to dry.

3. When the glue is completely dry, roll the half circle into a cone, overlapping the poster board until there is a point at the top of the hat. Staple together (Fig. 3).

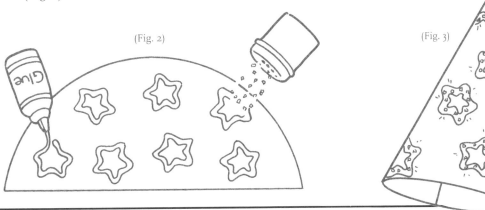

(Fig. 2)

(Fig. 3)

St. Lucia's Crown

You Will Need

Measuring tape   Tracing paper

White poster board   Green poster board

Scissors   Crayons or markers

Pencil   Stapler

What to Do

1. Measure the child's head.

2. Cut out a piece of white poster board that measures 6" high x the measurement of the child's head plus 3" lengthwise. With a pencil, draw a line about 2 1/2" up from the bottom of this piece of poster board (Fig. 1).

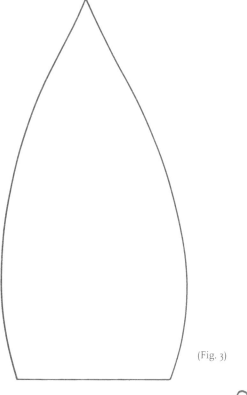

(Fig. 3)

(Fig. 1)

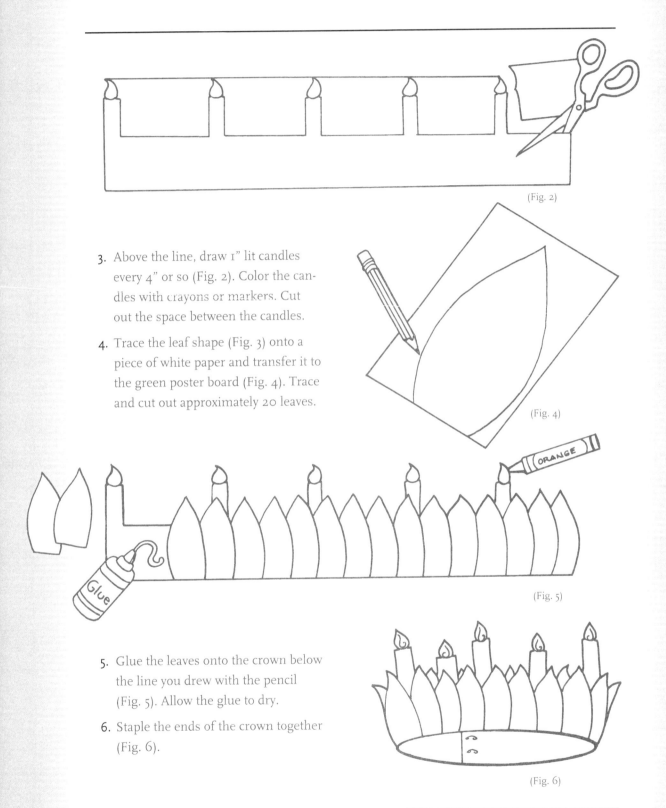

(Fig. 2)

3. Above the line, draw 1" lit candles every 4" or so (Fig. 2). Color the candles with crayons or markers. Cut out the space between the candles.

4. Trace the leaf shape (Fig. 3) onto a piece of white paper and transfer it to the green poster board (Fig. 4). Trace and cut out approximately 20 leaves.

(Fig. 4)

ORANGE

Glue

(Fig. 5)

5. Glue the leaves onto the crown below the line you drew with the pencil (Fig. 5). Allow the glue to dry.

6. Staple the ends of the crown together (Fig. 6).

(Fig. 6)

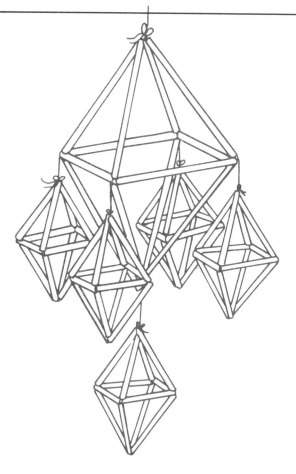

Himmeli

You Will Need

Spool of white thread

Ruler

Scissors

Needle

Forty-two 6" white drinking straws

What to Do

1. Cut a piece of thread 30" long. Thread the needle with this thread.

2. Bring the needle through four of the straws. Tie the ends of the thread together to make a tight diamond shape (Fig.1). Set aside and repeat two more times so that you have three diamond shapes.

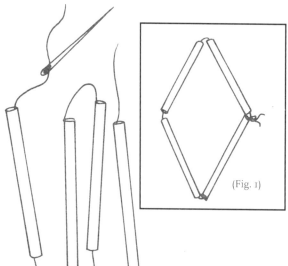

(Fig. 1)

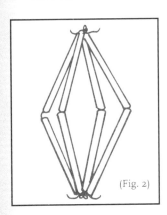

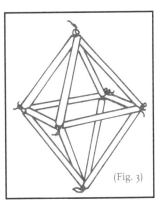

(Fig. 2)

(Fig. 3)

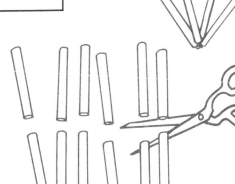

3. Bind two of the diamond shapes together using thread (Fig. 2). Slip the third diamond shape over the other two and use thread to bind this shape to the others (Fig. 3).

4. Cut a piece of thread 4" long. Tie this piece of thread to the top of the himmeli to use as a hanger. Find a place to hang the himmeli so that you can continue to add to it.

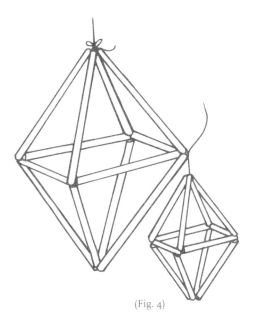

(Fig. 4)

5. Cut six straws exactly in half. Use these straws to make a smaller version of the shape you made in Steps 1 and 2. Repeat four more times, so that you have five smaller shapes.

6. Cut five pieces of thread 8" long. Tie one end of each of these threads to the four angles of the himmeli and to the bottom of the himmeli. Thread the needle with one of these threads and then bring the needle through the top of one of the smaller straw shapes several times (Fig. 4). Repeat with the other four threads and shapes.

7. Hang your himmeli where everyone can see and enjoy it.

Ice Lantern

You Will Need

Water

Large metal mixing bowl

Plastic 8 oz. yogurt container

Handful of small stones or pennies

Votive candle

Matches*

What to Do

1. Pour a couple of inches of water into the mixing bowl. Place the bowl outside or in the freezer to freeze.

2. Fill the yogurt container with the stones or pennies. Center the container on the ice in the bowl. Slowly pour more water into the bowl, so that it nearly reaches the rim of the yogurt container (Fig. 1). Return it outside or to the freezer to freeze solid (Fig. 2).

(Fig. 1)

(Fig. 2)

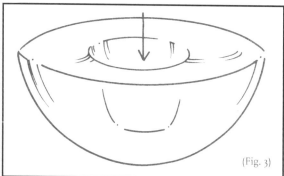

(Fig. 3)

3. To remove the lantern from its mold, run warm water on the outside of the bowl; the ice should slip out. Next remove the stones or pennies from the inner container and pour in warm water to loosen it.

4. Remove the container and place a votive candle (Fig. 3) in the opening. Light the candle for a beautiful ice lantern.

*This project should be done with adult supervision.

Finnish Carols

Hiljaa, Hiljaa Joulun Kellot Kajahtaa   Silently, Silently Christmas Bells Are Ringing

Hil - jaa,   hil - jaa   jou - lun kel - lot   ka - jah - taa.   Kaut - ta a - va -

ruuk - si - en   kai - kuu lau - lu   rie - mui -nen: Jee - sus tul - lut   on!

1. Hiljaa, hiljaa
   joulun kellot kajahtaa.
   Kautta a va ruuk si en
   kaikuu laulu riemuinen
   Jeesus tullut on!

2. Hiljaa, hiljaa
   joulun kellot kajahtaa.
   Taivahalla säteillen
   välkkyy sarja tähtösten:
   Jeesus tullut on!

3. Hiljaa, hiljaa
   joulun kellot kajahtaa.
   Kirkkaat joulukynttilät
   lempeästi hymyyvät:
   Jeesus tullut on!

4. Hiljaa, hiljaa
   joulun kellot kajahtaa.
   Kaikuu laulu lapsosten
   kirkkahasti helkkyen:
   Jeesus tullut on!

1. Silently, silently,
   Christmas bells are ringing,
   Through the wide open spaces
   a joyful song sounds:
   Jesus has arrived.

2. Silently, silently,
   Christmas bells are ringing,
   Radiating in the sky,
   a set of stars twinkling:
   Jesus has arrived.

3. Silently, silently,
   Christmas bells are ringing,
   Bright Christmas candles
   smiling sweetly:
   Jesus has arrived.

4. Silently, silently,
   Christmas bells are ringing,
   Children's song echoing,
   brightly ringing:
   Jesus has arrived.

Kun Maass' On Hanki   When Snow Covers the Ground

Kun maass' on han - ki___ ja jär - vet jääs - sä ja sil - mä sam -

mu - nut au - rin - gon   kun pääs - ky pit - kän on mat - kan pääs - sä ja

met - sä au - ti - o lau - lu - ton,   käy läm - min hen - kä - ys

tal - vi - sääs - sä. kun jou - lu on,___ kun jou - - lu on!___

1. Kun maass' on hanki ja järvet jäässa ja
   silmä sammunut auringon.
   kun pääsky pitkän on matkan päässä
   ja metsä autio lauluton,
   käy lämmin henkäys talvisäässa.
   kun joulu on, kun joulu on!

2. Ei huolta, murhetta kenkään muista,
   ei tunnu pakkaset tuikeat,
   vain laulu kaikuvi lasten suista
   ja silmät riemusta hehkuvat,
   ja liekit loistavat joulupuista,
   kun joulu on, kun joulu on!

3. On äiti laittanut kystä kyllä,
   hän lahjat antaa ja lahjat saa,
   vaan seimi, pahnat ja tähti yllä
   ne silmiin kalleina kangastaa;
   siks' mieli hellä on kristityllä,
   kun joulu on, kun joulu on!

1. When snow covers the ground and the
   lakes are frozen,
   and the eye of the sun has closed,
   When the swallow is far away and the forest
   is empty without a song,
   There is a warm breath in the winter air.
   It's Christmas, it's Christmas.

2. Nobody remembers a worry or sadness,
    nobody feels the cold.
   There's a song in children's mouths and
   their eyes are sparkling,
   And the candles are burning on the
   Christmas trees.
   It's Christmas, it's Christmas.

3. Mother has done plenty of cooking.
   She gives gifts and receives them.
   Only the manger, the straw, and the star above
   will shine preciously in your eyes,
   That's why a Christian feels love.
   It's Christmas, it's Christmas.

Finnish Recipes

Salted Salmon

2 tbsp. salt

2 tsp. sugar

1 lb. salmon fillets

2 tbsp. dried dill

In a small bowl, combine salt and sugar. Lightly rub the mixture onto the salmon fillets. Spread the rest of the salt and sugar mixture onto the bottom of a 9-inch x 9-inch square glass baking dish.

Lay the salmon fillets on top of the mixture and then sprinkle the dill on top of the salmon. Cover the dish with plastic wrap and allow to sit in the refrigerator for 24 hours.

To serve the salmon, slice thinly on the diagonal.

Makes 6 servings.

Pasty

1 1/2 cups rye flour

1 1/2 cups all-purpose
   flour

1 tsp. salt

1 cup shortening

1/2-2/3 cup water

1/2 lb. raw beef,
   finely minced

1 large potato, diced

1/2 cup carrot, diced

1/2 cup celery, diced

1 small onion, chopped

1/4 cup beef gravy

1 tbsp. butter

Preheat oven to 350°F. Combine flours and salt and cut in shortening with a pastry knife until mixture is like meal.

Stir in water, a little at a time, until a stiff dough forms. Shape the dough into 6 small balls. On a lightly floured surface, roll out the balls into 7-inch circles.

For the filling, combine the beef, vegetables, and gravy. Spread about 1/4 cup onto half of each circle to within 1/2 inch of the edge. Dot with a bit of butter. Brush the edge of other half with water, fold over, and seal. Cut a tiny slit in the top to allow steam to escape. Bake at 350°F for 30 minutes.

Makes 6 servings.

Liver Casserole

2 cups water
1 cup rice, uncooked
1 small onion, chopped
1 tbsp. butter or margarine
3/4 lb. ground liver
1/2 cup molasses
1 tsp. ginger

1 tsp. marjoram
1/4 tsp. white pepper
1/2 cup raisins
1/4 cup milk
1 egg
butter or margarine
lingonberry jam

In a medium saucepan, bring the water to a boil. Stir in the rice, cover, reduce heat, and simmer for 20 minutes.

Meanwhile, in a frying pan, sauté the onion in the butter or margarine until transparent.

Coat a casserole dish with cooking spray. In the casserole dish, mix together the cooked rice, onion, liver, molasses, ginger, marjoram, white pepper, raisins, milk, and egg. Top with a few dabs of butter. Bake at 350°F for 45 minutes to an hour. Serve with lingonberry jam.

Makes 6 servings.

Potato Casserole

2 lbs. medium red potatoes,
   unpeeled
2 tbsp. flour
1 tbsp. granulated sugar

2 tsp. salt
1 1/2 cups milk
1 tbsp. butter

Place the potatoes in a large saucepan. Cover with water and boil until tender when pierced with a fork. Drain. Peel the potatoes, and then mash them in a large bowl. While the mashed potatoes are still warm, mix in the flour. Cover the bowl with plastic wrap and allow to stand at room temperature for 3 to 4 hours.

Add the sugar, salt, milk, and butter to the potatoes. Coat a casserole dish with cooking spray and pour in the potato mixture. Bake at 350°F for 1 to 2 hours.

Makes 6 to 8 servings.

Christmas Glögg

1 bottle red wine
3 tbsp. Madeira
1/2 cup granulated sugar
1/3 cup raisins
1 cinnamon stick

6 whole cloves
1 tbsp. grated orange rind
1/4 cup blanched, slivered
    almonds
1/4 cup vodka (optional)

In a large saucepan over medium heat, combine all the ingredients except the vodka. Heat slowly, until steaming hot, stirring occasionally. Do not allow the glögg to boil. Before serving, add vodka if you wish. Serve warm.

Makes 6 servings.

Christmas Tarts

2 sticks butter or margarine,
    softened
1 1/4 cups flour
1/2 cup cold water

1 tsp. vinegar
About 1 cup plum jam
1 egg, beaten

In a large bowl, mix together the butter or margarine, flour, water, and vinegar to form a soft dough. Knead the dough for about 5 minutes. Place the dough in the refrigerator to harden, at least 1 hour.

Roll out the dough onto a lightly floured surface. Fold the dough a few times to make a puff pastry. Then roll the dough to about 1-inch thickness. Using a small glass or round cookie cutter dipped in flour, cut the dough into circles. Place about 1/2 teaspoon of plum jam in the middle of each circle, then fold the circles in half. Place the tarts on a cookie sheet. Brush with egg. Bake at 375 °F for about 12 minutes, or until light brown.

Makes about 24 tarts

Ginger Cookies

3/4 cup butter

1 cup granulated sugar

1 egg

1/4 cup dark molasses

1 tsp. ground cinnamon

1 tsp. ground ginger

1 tsp. ground cloves

1 1/2 teaspoons orange zest

2 cups flour, sifted

2 tsp. baking soda

In a large bowl, cream together the butter and 1 cup granulated sugar. Add the egg, molasses, cinnamon, ginger, cloves, orange zest, flour, and baking soda. Beat well. Form the dough into 1-inch balls. Roll in granulated sugar. Place 2 inches apart on a greased cookie sheet. Bake at 350°F for 10 to 12 minutes. Allow to cool on a wire rack. Makes about 3 dozen cookies.

Cinnamon Buns

1 tsp. dry yeast

3/4 cup warm milk

2 eggs, beaten separately

1 tsp. salt

1/2 cup granulated sugar

2 tsp. crushed cardamom

2 cups flour

2 sticks butter or margarine, softened

sugar

cinnamon

1 cup almonds or other nuts (optional)

In a large bowl, dissolve the yeast in the warm milk. Let sit for 5 minutes. Add one of the eggs, salt, sugar, cardamom, and flour. Mix well. Add one stick of the butter or margarine. Knead the dough until it is soft and elastic, about 10 minutes.

Cover the dough and let rise in a warm place for about 1 hour or until doubled in size. Punch down the dough and let sit for 5 minutes.

Turn the dough onto a floured surface and roll to about a 2-inch thickness. Spread the dough with the other stick of softened butter or margarine. Sprinkle with sugar and cinnamon. Add a layer of chopped almonds or other nuts, if desired. Roll up the dough and pinch the ends closed. Cut into 3- to 4-inch slices. Arrange the slices on a baking sheet covered with waxed paper. Cover and let rise in a warm place until doubled in size, about 30 minutes.

Brush the rolls with beaten egg and bake at 350°F for about 15 to 20 minutes. Makes about 8 buns.

Finnish Doughnuts

1 tsp. dry yeast
3/4 cup warm milk
1 egg, slightly beaten
1 tsp. salt
1/2 cup granulated sugar

2 tsp. crushed cardamom
1 3/4 cups flour
1 stick butter or margarine, softened
vegetable oil
confectioners' sugar

In a large bowl, dissolve the yeast in the warm milk. Let sit for 5 minutes. Add the egg, salt, granulated sugar, cardamom, and flour. Mix well. Add the butter or margarine. Knead the dough until it is soft and elastic, about 10 minutes.

Cover the dough and let rise in a warm place for about 1 hour or until doubled in size. Punch down the dough and let sit for 5 minutes.

Pinch off pieces of dough and form them into small rolls. Place on a cookie sheet, cover, and allow to rise in a warm place until doubled in size, about 30 minutes.

In a deep frying pan, pour in enough oil until it is about 2 inches deep. Heat the oil until very hot. Cook the doughnuts in the oil for about 15 minutes, or until golden brown, turning them halfway through the cooking time. Drain the doughnuts on paper towels. Roll in confectioners' sugar while they are still hot.

Makes about 25 doughnuts

Strawberry Snow

2 cups fresh strawberries or two
    10 oz. packages frozen whole
    strawberries, defrosted and
    drained
1/2 cup sugar

4 egg whites
pinch of salt
3/4 cup heavy cream, whipped
12 to 16 whole strawberries, fresh
    or frozen

With the back of a large spoon, rub the fresh or defrosted strawberries through a fine sieve into a small bowl. Stir the sugar into the puree a little at a time. With a wire whisk, beat the egg whites and salt vigorously in a large bowl until the whites are stiff but not dry.

Gently fold the strawberry puree into the egg whites. Then gently fold in the whipped cream. Pour the strawberry snow into individual serving bowls, and garnish with the whole strawberries. The snow can be served at once, or it may be refrigerated for a few hours and served later in the day.

Makes 6 servings.

Glossary

Åbo (AH boh) Swedish name for the city of Turku.

Ahvenanmaa (AH ven an MAY) Finnish name for Åland.

Åland Islands (OH land) islands in the Gulf of Bothnia.

Aleksanterinkatu (a liks AHN ter in KA too) Helsinki's Christmas street.

Alvar Aalto (AL ver AHL toh) architect of Rovaniemi.

Annikki (AN ik ee) a familiar name for St. Ann.

Arktikum (ARK ti koom) museum in Rovaniemi.

Blomqvist (BLOOM kwist) Professor Alexander Blomqvist's German wife is credited with having the first Finnish Christmas tree.

Brinkkala (BRINK ah lah) Brinkkala House, where the Proclamation of Christmas Peace is read.

En etsi valtaa loistoa (en ET si VAL tah LOIST ah) "Christmas Prayer," a traditional Finnish Christmas carol.

Enkeli taivaan (EN kel i TIE van) "Heavenly Angel," a traditional Finnish Christmas carol.

Enontekio (en on TEK i oh) city in Lapland.

Folkhälsan (fohlk HEL sun) health organization that co-sponsors the Lucia competition.

glögg (glug) Swedish Christmas drink.

glögi (GLUG ee) Finnish adaptation of Swedish glogg.

Hauskaa Joulua (HOW skuh YOH luh) "Merry Christmas."

himmeli (HIM el ee) geometric mobile made from straw as a Christmas decoration.

Hufvudstadsbladet (hoo vood STAHDZ blahd it) Finland's principal Swedish-language newspaper; co-sponsor of the Lucia competition.

Inari (IN ah ree) city in Lapland.

Ivalo (EE vahl oh) city in Lapland.

jouluhauki (yoh loo HOW kee) Christmas pike.

joulukolkutus (yoh loo KOHL koo tus) Christmas knock on the door by Joulupukki.

Joulupukki (yoh loo POO kee) Finnish "Santa Claus," literally "Yule Buck."

joulusauna (yoh loo SOW nuh) Christmas sauna.

joulutortut (yoh loo TOHR tut) Christmas prune turnovers.

Kemi (KEM ee) city on the Gulf of Bothnia.

Klinckowstrom (KLINK oh strum) Helsinki nobleman Baron Klinckowstrom is said to have had eight Christmas trees in his home in 1829.

Korvatunturi (kohr vuh TOON ter ee) Korvatunturi Fell, or "Ear Mountain," is where Santa lives in eastern Lapland.

korvapuustit (kohr vuh POO stit) pastries.

kota (KOH tuh) traditional Sami dwelling.

limppu (LIM poo) Christmas loaf decorated with shapes cut from gingerbread dough.

loppiainen (loh pee EYE nun) Epiphany.

löyly (LOH luh) steamy sauna atmosphere.

mankara (MAHN kuh ruh) "Lifting the Mankara" is a fortune-telling party game played at New Year's.

Mariehamn (MAHR ee uh hahm) city on the Åland Islands.

markka (MAHR kuh) unit of money.

Markus Rautio (MAR koos ROW tee oh) "Uncle Markus" on the radio.

nakkovaika (noh kuv EYE kuh) old name for Christmas, literally "throw time."

Napapiiri (NAH pah pee ree) town outside of Rovaniemi where Santa's Workshop Village is located.

nuuttipukit (noo tee POO keet) Canute goats.

olkikruunu (ohl kee KROO noo) straw crown.

Onnellista Uutta Vuotta (oh nel EES tuh OOT uh VWOHT uh) "Happy New Year."

Oulu (OH loo) city on the Gulf of Bothnia.

Pietarsaari (pee ET ahr sahr ee) first city in Finland to have a decorated Christmas tree in its town square.

pikkujoulu (PIK yoo ow loo) "Little Christmas."

piparkakut (pi pahr KAH koot) gingerbread cookies.

pulla (POOL ah) braided coffeebread.

Ranua (RAH noo ah) Ranua Zoo is in Lapland.

Rauma (ROW mah) city on the Gulf of Bothnia.

Rovaniemi (ROH van ee em ee) city in Lapland.

sahti (SAH tee) home-brewed beer.

Salla (SAHL uh) town near Rovaniemi where Salla Reindeer Park is located.

Sami (SAHM ee) the nomadic people who live in Lapland.

Samppalinna (sahm puh LEE nuh) Samppalinna Hill is where fireworks are set off at New Year's in Turku.

Senaatintori (SEN ah tin tohr ee) Senaatintori Square is the area of Helsinki where the national New Year's party is held.

Silja (SIL yee uh) a large ferry line.

sisu (SIS oo) the Finnish quality of endurance against all odds.

Staalu (STAHL oo) witch of Lapland.

Syvävaara (SIV uh vahr uh) Syvavaara Fell is the mountain where Santapark is located.

tapaninpäivä (TOP an in pie vuh) St. Stephen's Day, December 26.

Tuomaan markkinat (TOO oh mahn MARK in aht) Thomas's Market in Helsinki's Esplanade Park.

Turku (TOOR koo) Finnish name for the city of Åbo.

vihta (VIT uh) little whisk of birch twigs.

Acknowledgments

Cover   ©Matti Kolho, Lehtikuva Oy

2   ©Matti Kolho, Kuvasuomi Ky

5   ©Soile Kallio, Lehtikuva Oy

6   ©Matti Kolho, Kuvasuomi Ky

8   ©Soile Kallio, Lehtikuva Oy

10   ©Matti Kolho, Kuvasuomi Ky

11   ©Sari Gustafsson, Lehtikuva Oy

13-17   ©Matti Kolho, Kuvasuomi Ky

18   National Museum of Finland, Helsinki; ©Matti Kolho, Lehtikuva Oy

20-21   ©Matti Kolho, Kuvasuomi Ky

22   ©Jonny Holmen, Lehtikuva Oy; ©Matti Kuvasuomi Ky

23   Martti Puhakka, Turku Provincial Museum, Finland

24-26   ©Matti Kolho, Kuvasuomi Ky

27   ©Heikki Saukkomaa, Lehtikuva Oy; ©Matti Kolho, Kuvasuomi Ky

29   ©Matti Kolho, Kuvasuomi Ky; ©Soile Kallio, Lehtikuva Oy

30-33   ©Matti Kolho, Kuvasuomi Ky

34   National Museum of Finland, Helsinki

35-37   ©Matti Kolho, Kuvasuomi Ky

38   ©Bryan & Cherry Alexander

40   ©Martti Kainulainen, Lehtikuva Oy

41   ©Kimo Mantyla, Lehtikuva Oy

42   ©Matti Kainulainen, Lehtikuva Oy

43   ©Matti Kainulainen, Lehtikuva Oy; ©Matti Bjorkman, Lehtikuva Oy

44   ©Matti Kolho, Kuvasuomi Ky

45   ©Nik Wheeler; ©Matti Kolho, Kuvasuomi Ky

46   ©Martti Kainulainen, Lehtikuva Oy

48-50   ©Matti Kolho, Kuvasuomi Ky

51   ©Nik Wheeler

52-55   ©Matti Kolho, Kuvasuomi Ky

56   ©Bryan & Cherry Alexander

57-58   ©Matti Kolho, Kuvasuomi Ky

60   National Museum of Finland, Helsinki; ©Matti Kolho, Kuvasuomi Ky

61   ©Pekka Sakki, Lehtikuva Oy

62-64   ©Matti Kolho, Kuvasuomi Ky

Craft Illustrations: Laura D'Argo*

Recipe Cards: WORLD BOOK photos by Dale DeBolt*

Advent Calendar: ©Bryan & Cherry Alexander

Advent Calendar illustrations: Laura D'Argo*

All entries marked with an asterisk (*) denote illustration created exclusively for World Book, Inc.